FOOD TECHNOLOGY RECIPES

2nd Edition

Contents:

Muffins:

Carrot Muffins   p3
American Muffins   p4
Breakfast muffins   p5

Cakes

Fairy cakes   p6
Rock cakes   p7
Cinnamon tea ring   p8
Cake making methods   p9
  •   Rubbing in
  •   Creaming
  •   Whisking
  •   Melting
Microwave chocolate cake   p10

Biscuits

Fruit biscuits   p11
Maryland cookies   p12
Gingerbread men   p13
Shortbread   p13
Creaming method   p14
  ▪   Shrewsbury biscuit
  ▪   Easter biscuit
  ▪   Dundee biscuit
  ▪   Piped Biscuit

Other desserts

Cereal bar   p15
Flap jack   p16

Scones   p17
Chocolate brownies   p18
Jam Tarts   p19
Mince pies   p20
Apple crumble   p21
Chocolate log   p22
Fruit salad   p23
Baked Alaska   p24

Drinks

Chocolate milkshake   p25
Banana smoothie   p26

Main Dishes:

Bolognese sauce   p27
Chicken curry   p28
Chicken tikka masala   p29
Chinese stir fry   p30
Christmas Jalousie   p31
Italian smoked fish   p32
Lasagne - Meat sauce   p33
Lasagne – Cheese sauce   p34
Lasagne – Assembly   p35
Parmesan chicken nuggets   p36
Shepard's pie   p37

Cold side dishes:

Pasta salad   p38
Coleslaw   p39

Dough recipes

Bread – Simple   p40
Pizza   p41

Carrot Muffins

Ingredients:

280g Self raising flour
5g (1 tsp) Bicarbonate of soda
½ tsp of salt
10g (2 tsp) ground cinnamon
1 egg
150g brown sugar
120 ml milk
340g grated carrot
85g butter
50g raisins

Equipment:

- Mixing Bowl x 2
- Teaspoon
- Measuring jug
- Fork
- Grater
- Muffin tin/Cases

Method:

1. Set oven to 190oC. Place muffin cases in tray.

2. Grate the carrot finely.

3. Sift the flour, bicarbonate of soda, salt and cinnamon together into a large bowl.

4. In a separate bowl mix the egg, milk, sugar carrot, raisins and butter together.

5. Pour all of the liquid mixture into the dry ingredients. Stir until combined. Do not over-stir.

6. Fill muffin cup only ¾ full and back for 25 – 30 minutes until firm to touch and golden brown. **Makes 12 muffins..**

7. Wash dry and put away all equipment used. Tidy sink and work surface. Wipe surface with a soapy cloth.

8. Remove muffins using an oven glove. Cool on a wire rack. Wash and dry muffin tray.

American muffins

Makes 10 muffins

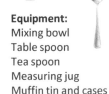

Equipment:
Mixing bowl
Table spoon
Tea spoon
Measuring jug
Muffin tin and cases
Weighing scales

Ingredients:
250g self raising flour
1 teaspoon baking powder
½ teaspoon salt
100g sugar
85g sultanas, chocolate chips or blueberries
250ml milk
80ml oil
1 egg

Method:

1. Light oven to 160°C.
2. Prepare muffin tin with ten paper cases.
3. Measure out all of the ingredients and place them into the mixing bowl.
4. Mix all ingredients together with a table spoon until thoroughly mixed.
5. Divide the mixture **evenly** between the muffin cases.
6. Bake for 20 – 25 minutes.

muffins are ready when the top springs back when lightly pressed and are lightly brown in colour.

Breakfast Muffins

Ingredients:
- 175g Self Raising Flour
- 50g Porridge Oats
- 140g Soft Brown Sugar
- 2 teaspoon ground cinnamon
- $\frac{1}{2}$ teaspoon Bicarbonate of Soda
- 1 teaspoon of vanilla extract
- 150ml Milk
- 6 tablespoon Oil
- 1 Egg
- 175g Sultanas

Equipment:
- Mixing Bowl
- Tablespoon
- Measuring Jug
- Fork
- Muffin Tin/Cases

Method:
1. Light oven 180°C
2. Prepare muffin tin with ten paper cases
3. Put flour, oats, sugar, cinnamon and bicarbonate of soda in a large bowl
4. Rub all ingredients through your fingers as if making pastry
5. Beat the egg, then stir in the milk, vanilla and oil
6. Lightly stir the egg mix into the flour
7. Fold the sultanas into the mixture
8. Divide between the paper cases and bake for 20 – 25 minutes

Fairy Cakes

Ingredients:

- 50g Soft Margarine
- 50g Self Raising Flour
- 50g Castor Sugar
- 1 Egg

Equipment:

- Mixing bowl
- Electric Whisk
- Plate
- Tablespoon, Teaspoon and Knife
- Spatula
- Patty Tin and Cake Cases

Method:

1. Light oven 180°C
2. Put cake cases into patty tin
3. Break egg on plate to check it
4. Put ingredients into a bowl and whisk on low power until flour is mixed in
5. Scrape the sides with the spatula and mix again until soft and creamy
6. Place 1 heaped teaspoon of mixture into each pastry case
7. Bake in oven for 10 – 15 minutes
8. Place on cooling rack to cool
9. Once cool ice with butter cream and jam to make Butterfly Cakes

Rock Cakes

Ingredients:

- 50g Margarine
- 100g Self Raising Flour
- 50g Mixed Dried Fruit
- 50g Granulated Sugar
- ½ teaspoon Mixed Spice
- 1 Egg

Equipment:

- Baking Sheet
- Large Mixing Bowl
- Small Mixing Bowl
- Sieve
- Teaspoon
- Fork

Method:

1. Light oven 200°C and grease a baking sheet
2. Sieve flour and spice into a large bowl
3. Rub in margarine until it resembles breadcrumbs
4. Stir in sugar and dried fruit
5. Beat egg and mix in with fork to form a firm but sticky dough
6. Place heaped teaspoon evenly on baking sheet and bake for 15 minutes or until golden brown
7. Place on cooling rack

Cinnamon Tea Ring

Method:

- Grease a 23 cm. baking tin.
- Put the flour in the bowl, stir in the salt and stir in the yeast
- Rub in the butter with your fingertips
- Add the egg and milk and mix together to form a dough
- Knead firmly for 10 minutes.Then roll out in to a rectangle 23cm X 30cm
- Cream together the butter, cinnamon and brown sugar until light and fluffy. Spread over the dough
- Place in the tin or divide in to 8 pieces.
- Roll up the dough and place in a ring shape in the tin
- When the dough has proven bake for 15 – 20 minutes @ 190°//Gas mark 5
- Brush with the syrup and leave to cool slightly

Ingredients:

225g Strong white flour
1 Sachet yeast
25g Butter
50g Softened butter
50g Soft brown sugar
2 tbsp Maple syrup
$\frac{1}{2}$ tsp salt
125ml Warm milk
1 Beaten egg
50g Sultanas

Cake making methods

Rubbing in - Method

Used for farmhouse fruit cake, raspberry buns, rock cakes

200g. plain flour   10ml. baking powder
100g. margarine   100g. caster sugar
2 eggs   30ml. milk
Flavouring ingredients : 175g. dried fruit or 75g. chocolate chips
Mixing : fat rubbed into the flour
Ratio: half or less than half fat to flour. Higher proportion of liquid
Raising agent: chemical baking powder or self-raising flour
Texture : dry, open, crumb

Creaming method

Used for Victoria Sandwich, Madeira cake, Dundee cake

100g. self-raising flour   100g. caster sugar
100g. soft margarine   2 eggs
Mixing: fat and sugar creamed together
Ratio: half or more than half fat to flour
Raising agent: chemical self-raising flour, air from creaming
Texture: fine, light, even

Melting method

Used for gingerbread, parkin, flapjacks, brownies

200g. plain flour   5ml. bicarbonate of soda
10ml. ground ginger   5ml. mixed spice
50g. soft brown sugar   100g. margarine
150g. golden syrup   125ml. milk
2 eggs   50g. golden syrup
Mixing: fat melted with treacle, syrup, and sugar
Ratio: half or less fat to flour. High proportion
Texture: moist, sticky, rich

Whisking - Method

Used for Swiss roll, sponge cake, sponge drops, sponge flan case

50g. caster sugar   50g. plain flour
2 eggs
Mixing: eggs and sugar whisked together
Ratio: equal proportions of sugar and flour to weight of eggs
Raising agent: air and steam from water in eggs
Texture: light, even, soft

Microwave chocolate cake

Ingredients:

½ tsp. baking powder
¾ tsp. baking soda
1 egg
125g. flour
1 tsp. vanilla essence

50 g. margarine
2 tsp. golden syrup
125g. sugar
125 ml. milk
2 Tbsp. Cocoa

Method:

1. Melt the margarine and golden syrup together in the microwave for 45 seconds.
2. When cool mix in the sugar and egg
3. Add flour, cocoa, baking powder, milk and vanilla,
4. Mix with a spoon pressing out any lumps.
5. Pour into a 20cm ring mould and cover with wax paper (this is very important to cover the tin well) and microwave for 4 mins on full power.
6. Cool on a rack.

Lemon/Orange/Fruit Biscuits

Ingredients:
- 100g Self Raising Flour
- 50g Butter/Margarine
- 50g Castor Sugar
- 1 Egg
- 1 teaspoon Lemon/Orange Rind
- 1 Teaspoon of Lemon/Orange Juice

Equipment:
- Baking Tray
- Large Bowl
- Small Bowl
- Teaspoon
- Palette Knife
- Rolling Pin
- Biscuit Cutter
- Grater

Method:
1. Light Oven 180°C, collect equipment and grease baking tray
2. Put flour and sugar into a large bowl, cut up the margarine and add
3. Rub into flour until it resembles breadcrumbs
4. Separate the egg and add the yolk to the mixture, add the juice and the rind
5. Mix into a smooth dough and knead slightly. Roll out thinly
6. Cut about 10 – 15 biscuits with a medium cutter
7. Place the biscuits on a baking tray, bake for 12 – 15 minutes
8. Place on a cooling tray

Maryland Cookies

Ingredients:
- 50g Castor Sugar
- 50g Soft Margarine
- 75g Plain Flour
- $\frac{1}{2}$ Teaspoon Syrup
- $\frac{1}{2}$ Tablespoon Milk
- $\frac{1}{2}$ level teaspoon Bicarbonate Soda
- 25g Chocolate Chips

Equipment:
- Mixing Bowl
- Wooden Spoon
- Fork
- Tablespoon
- Teaspoon
- Baking Sheet
- Cooling Rack

Method:
1. Light oven 180°C, collect ingredients and equipment
2. Cream margarine and sugar
3. Add flour
4. Melt syrup and milk, add bicarbonate soda
5. Add milk mixture to the margarine, sugar and flour
6. Add the chocolate chips and mix well
7. Place on a greased baking sheet and press down with a fork
8. Bake for 15 – 20 minutes until golden brown

Gingerbread men

100g/4oz self-raising flour,
1 level teaspoon ground ginger
¼ level teaspoon mixed spice
50g/2oz butter
40g/1.5oz caster sugar
1 level tablespoon melted golden syrup

Method
Sift flour, ginger and spice into bowl
Rub into butter finely
Add sugar. Mix to a very stiff paste with syrup and milk
Roll out thinly, cut into gingerbread men shapes
Transfer to buttered baking trays
Bake just above centre of moderate oven (180°C/350°F gas no.4) for 10 mins
Leave on trays for 1-2 mins before transferring to wire cooling rack
Store in airtight tin when cold

Shortbread

150g   Plain flour
100g   Margarine
50g   Caster sugar

Method
Place all ingredients into a mixing bowl and rub in with fingertips
Squeeze into a ball and knead until smooth
Shape into a circle or cut into rounds or fingers
Place on a greased baking tray
Bake in an oven at 160°C for 15-20 minutes or until golden brown

BISCUITS MADE BY THE CREAMING METHOD

INGREDIENTS	SHREWSBURY BISCUITS	EASTER BISCUITS	DUNDEE BISCUITS	PIPED BISCUITS
Flour	100 g (4 0Z)	100 g (4 oz)	100 g (1 oz) 25 g (1 oz) rice flour	100 g (4 oz)
Butter or margarine	50 g (2 oz)	50 g (2 oz)	75 g (3 oz)	75 g (3 oz)
Caster sugar	50 g (2 oz)	50 g (2 oz)	50 g (2 oz)	50 g (2 oz)
Egg	½ or 1 yolk	½ or 1 yolk	1 yolk	½ or 1 yolk
Other ingredients or special method	1 teaspoon grated lemon rind or ¼ teaspoon ground cinnamon or caraway. Cut in large rounds, or cut in 50-mm (2 inch) rounds, sandwich with jam and dredge the tops with icing sugar.	¼ teaspoon ground cinnamon or caraway and 25 g (1oz) currants.	Roll to 12 mm (1/2 inch), cut into fingers 25 by 50 mm (1 by 1 ½ inches) And roughen with a fork, drawn other them lengthways.	¼ teaspoon ground cinnamon. Pipe as stars and finish, When cold, and glace cherries or sandwich 2 with jam, or pipe as fingers and dip the ends with chocolate icing.

Oven temperature 170c gas no.3

1. Grease a baking tray
2. Follow the rubbing in method
3. Mix the ingredients to a dough, a little softer than short pastry.
4. Roll it to 3 to 5mm thick (1/8 –1/4 inch)
5. Cut into shapes with round or fancy cutters or cut them into neat fingers 25 by 50mm (1- 2 inches) ; carefully lift the biscuits without spoiling their shapes. Prick them with a fork or skewer.
6. Bake them until set and pale golden.

Cereal Bar

Ingredients:

- 125g Rolled Oats
- 75g Margarine
- 1 tablespoon Golden Syrup
- $\frac{1}{4}$ teaspoon spices and lemon rind
- 25g of each additional ingredient

Equipment:

- 1 Saucepan
- Wooden Spoon
- Spatula
- Tablespoon
- Baking tin

Method:

1. Heat oven to 200°C
2. Grease the tin
3. Prepare additional ingredients i.e. cut up
4. Put margarine and syrup into the saucepan and gently heat until margarine has melted
5. Add oats and additional ingredients and mix well
6. Press mixture into the greased tin and flatten with the spatula
7. Bake in the oven for 15 – 20 minutes
8. Cut into pieces with a knife and leave to cool
9. Once cool ease the cereal bars from the tin

Flapjack

Ingredients:
- 250g Rolled Oats
- 100g Sugar
- 100g Margarine
- 1 rounded tablespoon Golden Syrup

Equipment:
- Large Mixing Bowl
- Saucepan
- Wooden Spoon
- Spatula
- Tablespoon
- Swiss Roll Tin

Method:
1. Heat oven to 190°C
2. Grease the tin
3. Put the oats and sugar into a bowl and mix together
4. Put margarine and syrup into a saucepan and gently heat until the margarine has melted
5. Pour the syrup over the oats and mix well
6. Press the mixture into the greased tin and flatten with the spatula
7. Bake in oven for 15 - 20 minutes, until the mixture is golden brown and firm to touch
8. Cut into 8 or 12 pieces with a knife and leave to cool

Scones

Ingredients:

- 250g Self Raising Flour
- 50g Sugar
- 50g Margarine
- 50g Dried Fruit
- 125ml Skimmed Milk

Equipment:

- Baking Sheet
- Large Bowl
- Rolling Pin
- Knife
- Flour Dredger
- Cutter
- Cooling Rack

Method:

1. Light oven 220°C and grease baking sheet
2. Put Flour into large bowl
3. Rub the margarine and sugar into flour
4. Add the dried fruit
5. Mix in the milk quickly using a knife
6. Bring together with fingertips and place onto a floured surface
7. Roll out to 2cm thick, cut into 6-7 scones
8. Place on baking sheet and bake in the oven for 10 minutes until well risen and golden brown

Chocolate Brownies

Ingredients:
- 100g Soft Margarine
- 150g Plain/Milk Chocolate
- 100G Self Raising Flour
- 100g Castor Sugar
- 2 tablespoons Water
- 1 teaspoon Vanilla Essence
- 2 Eggs
- 50g Chopped Walnuts

Equipment:
- Large Glass Bowl
- Small Glass Bowl
- Fork
- Wooden Spoon
- Saucepan
- Teaspoon
- Sieve
- Measuring Jug
- Baking Tin

Method:
1. Light Oven 180°C
2. Grease baking tin with some margarine
3. Melt chocolate with margarine and water, over a gentle heat stirring all the time
4. Sieve the flour into a large bowl
5. Beat the eggs in the small bowl
6. Add the castor sugar and vanilla essence to the melted chocolate
7. Pour the chocolate mixture onto the flour and mix well
8. Add the eggs to the mixture and beat well
9. Fold in the nuts
10. Pour the mixture into the tin and make until risen and firm to touch

Jam Tarts

Ingredients:
- 75g Plain Flour
- 25g Wholemeal Flour
- 25g Lard
- 25 g Margarine
- 2 tablespoons Water
- 3 tablespoons Red Jam

Equipment:
- Mixing Bowl
- Palette Knife
- Sieve
- Measuring Jug
- Tablespoon
- Teaspoon
- Bun Tin

Method:
1. Light oven 220°C/Gas 7, collect ingredients and equipment
2. Sieve the flour, cut the fat and add
3. Rub the fat in quickly using fingertips
4. Add water and mix quickly and lightly into a firm dough
5. Turn onto a floured surface and knead gently to make smooth
6. Turn over and roll out thinly
7. Cut into rounds and line patty tin
8. Re-roll the rest of the pastry to make nine tarts
9. Place a teaspoon of jam into the centre of each pastry case and bake for 10 – 15 minutes

Mince Pies

Ingredients:
- 100g Plain Flour
- 25g Margarine
- 25g Lard
- 200g Mincemeat
- Pinch of Salt
- Cold Water

Equipment:
- Sieve
- Spreading Knife
- Mixing Bowl
- Tablespoon
- Rolling Pin
- Bun Tin
- Teaspoon
- Pastry Brush

Method:
1. Light oven 200°C/Gas 6
2. Sieve the flour and salt into a mixing bowl
3. Cut the fat into small pieces, add to the flour and rub in
4. Add coldwater a tablespoon at a time, until the mixture comes together in a ball, mixture should be smooth
5. Use a little flour to roll the pastry out, use round cutters for the base and lids of the pies
6. Line a greased bun tin with a pastry disc
7. Use a teaspoon to fill the pies with mincemeat – **Do Not Over Fill**
8. Dampen the edges of the pies and fix on the lids
9. Seal the edges
10. Cook in the oven for approximately 10 minutes until golden brown

Apple Crumble

Ingredients:

• 2 Cooking Apples, Peeled, Cored and Cooked

• 100g Plain Flour

• 50g Margarine

• 25g Sugar

Equipment:

• Mixing Bowl

• Tablespoon

• Spreading Knife

• Sieve

Method:

1. Light Oven 180°C
2. Peel and core the apples (keep them in water when not in use to stop them turning brown)
3. Cook apples with a tablespoon of sugar and water until soft
4. Sieve flour into mixing bowl
5. Cut margarine into small pieces with knife and add to flour
6. Rub margarine into flour
7. When the mixture looks like breadcrumbs, stir in the sugar
8. Spoon crumble topping onto the apples and place in the oven for about 20 minutes, or until golden brown

Chocolate Yule Log

Ingredients:

• Chocolate Swiss Roll

• 200g bar Dairy Milk/Plain Chocolate

Equipment:

- Glass Bowl
- Saucepan
- Tablespoon

Method:

1. Break chocolate into a glass bowl
2. Melt over a saucepan of hot not boiling water
3. Spoon over the Swiss roll
4. Make a pattern on the chocolate to resemble tree bark
5. Dust with icing sugar
6. Decorate with holy leaves, Berries or Robin

Fresh Fruit Salad

Ingredients:
- 1 Apple
- 1 Banana
- 1 Pear
- Small Carton of Juice/Small Tin of Fruit in Syrup

Two of the Following:
- 1 Kiwi Fruit
- 1 Mango
- 1 Passion Fruit
- 1 Tangerine or Satsuma
- A few Strawberries or Raspberries
- Lemon Juice

Equipment:
- Chopping Board
- Small Bowl
- Vegetable Knife

Method:
1. Peel or wash the fruit
2. Cut the fruit into even sized portions
3. Put apple and banana into lemon juice
4. Add juice or fruit syrup to bowl
5. Combine all reaming fruits and mix

Baked Alaska

Ingredients:

- 1 slice of Swiss Roll
- 1 Scoop of Vanilla Ice Cream
- 1 egg white
- 40g Castor Sugar

Equipment:

- Mixing bowl
- Electric Whisk
- Tablespoon
- Baking Sheet

Method:

1. Light oven 220°C
2. Separate the egg
3. Whisk the white until it forms a peak
4. Whisk in 1 tablespoon of sugar
5. Fold in remaining sugar
6. Place a scoop of ice cream on the slice of Swiss Roll (do this on baking sheet)
7. Cover the Swiss Roll and ice cream completely with the meringue mixture
8. Bake for a couple of minutes in the oven

Chocolate Milkshake

Ingredients:

- 200ml Semi Skimmed Milk
- 1 level tablespoon Drinking Chocolate
- 1 tablespoon low fat Ice Cream
- Whipped Cream to decorate

Equipment:

- Glass
- Small Bowl
- Tablespoon
- Jug
- Liquidiser

Method:

1. Collect equipment
2. Measure the milk
3. Put the drinking chocolate into the small bowl and blend together with two tablespoons of milk, until smooth
4. Pour the rest of the milk into the bowl, then into the liquidiser, with the ice cream
5. Liquidise until frothy
6. Pour into the glass
7. Decorate with cream

Banana Smoothie

Ingredients:

- 200ml Semi-Skimmed Milk
- 1 Banana
- 1 teaspoon Clear Honey

Equipment:
- Jug
- Glass
- Teaspoon
- Straw
- Blender

Method:
1. Place all the ingredients in the blender
2. Blend until smooth
3. Pour into a tall glass, serve with a straw

Bolognese Sauce

Ingredients:
- 250 – 500g Minced Meat (Beef/Lamb/Turkey)
- 1 Onion
- 1 Tin Chopped Tomatoes
- 2 tablespoons of Tomato Puree
- 1 Oxo Cube
- $\frac{1}{2}$ Teaspoon Basil
- $\frac{1}{2}$ Teaspoon Oregano
- 1 Clove of Garlic
- 2 teaspoons of paprika
- 3 Mushrooms (Optional)

Equipment:
- Large Saucepan
- Wooden Spoon
- Chopping Board
- Sharp Knife
- Plate

Method:
1. Collect equipment
2. Peel and finely dice the onion
3. Slice the mushrooms
4. Place the onions and meat in the saucepan and cook on a medium heat until the meat is brown
5. Add the tin of chopped tomatoes, tomato puree, mushrooms, stock cube, herbs and seasoning
6. Mix thoroughly, add some water if needed, and bring to the boil
7. Simmer for 15 minutes

Simple Chicken curry

Ingredients:
- 2tbs oil
- 2 small onions
- 250g chicken
- 1 clove garlic
- 1 tsp ginger
- 1 tbs curry powder/paste
- 50g creamed coconut
- 2 tbs fresh coriander (optional)

Equipment:
- Saucepan
- Sharp Knife
- Chopping Board
- Wooden Spoon

Method:
1. Prepare all vegetables and dice the chicken
2. Heat oil in saucepan and add onion and garlic, cook until soft, add all other vegetables.
1. Stir in the curry powder and ginger and coriander.
2. Add the chicken, cook until well done.
3. Add the coconut cream and stock.
4. Simmer gently for 20 mins
5. Serve with rice and vegetables

Chicken Tikka Masala

Ingredients:
- 2 tablespoons Oil
- 1 Onion
- 250g Chicken or Turkey Breast
- 2 teaspoons Tikka Paste
- 1 teaspoon Tandoori Paste (optional)
- 150ml Water
- Small carton Single Cream or Yoghurt

Equipment:
- Large Saucepan
- Knife
- Chopping Board
- Teaspoon
- Measuring Jug
- Wooden Spoon

Method:
1. Heat the oil in a large pan. Peel chop and fry the onion.
2. Cut the chicken into small cubes or strips and fry for five minutes, stirring, until it is all white in colour
3. Stir in the pastes and fry for 2 minutes. Add the water, bring to the boil, and simmer with the lid on for 10 – 15 minutes. Turn off the heat and stir in the cream.
4. Serve on a bed of rice, sprinkle with fresh coriander

Chinese Stir Fry

Ingredients:
- 1 portion of Egg Noodles
- 1 tablespoon Oil
- 1 tablespoon Soy Sauce
- Selection of 4 Vegetables i.e. Carrot, Beansprouts, Corn, Cabbage, French Beans, Cauliflower, Broccoli, Peppers etc.

Equipment:
- Saucepan
- Sharp Knife
- Chopping Board
- Wok
- Wooden Spoon

Method:
1. Boil enough water to cover the noodles. When water is boiling add the noodles and cook for the required time
2. Prepare the vegetables
3. Drain the noodles in a colander
4. Put oil in the wok. Add the vegetables and fry on a medium heat for three minutes. Add the soy sauce
5. Stir in the noodles
6. Place in a container

Christmas Jalousie

Ingredients:

- 250g Puff Pastry
- 3 tablespoons Sweet Mincemeat
- Icing Sugar to decorate

Equipment:

- Rolling Pin
- Table Knife
- Flour Dredger
- Tablespoon
- Pastry Brush

Method:

1. Light the oven 220°C, collect equipment and ingredients
2. Roll pastry into a large square, trim edges and cut in half
3. Put one half onto the baking tray and fold the other in half
4. Make cuts on the folded edge of the pastry, about 1 cm apart
5. Wet edges of the pastry on the baking sheet and spoon on the mincemeat, leaving the edges clear
6. Place the other pastry on top to form the lid
7. Seal the edges by pressing down lightly to sick them together
8. Knock up the edges with table knife, to help pastry puff up
9. Brush the top of the pastry with beaten egg
10. Bake in the oven to golden brown and risen

Coleslaw

Ingredients:

- ¼ White Cabbage
- 1 Carrot
- 1 Small Onion
- 2 Tablespoons Mayonnaise

Equipment:

- Food Processor
- Spatula
- Tablespoon
- Mixing Bowl

Method:

1. Wash the Carrot
2. Take the outside leaves off the cabbage
3. Peel and quarter the onion
4. Use the processors shredding tool for the cabbage, grating tool for the carrot and the chopping tool for the onion
5. Combine the prepared vegetables with the mayonnaise
6. Garnish with parsley and serve

Italian Smoked Fish

Ingredients:
- 450g Smoked Cod, Haddock, Tinned Tuna or Crab Sticks
- 1 Dessertspoon (10ml Oil)
- 1 Small Onion
- 1 Red Pepper, deseeded and chopped
- 75g Button Mushrooms, halved
- 125g low fat soft cheese with garlic and herbs
- 100ml Milk
- 100g Cooked Pasta
- Fresh Chopped Parsley to garnish

Equipment:
- Large Saucepan
- Wooden spoon
- Tablespoon
- Sharp Knife
- Chopping Board

Method

1. Cut the onion pepper and mushrooms and cook for 3 – 4 minutes in saucepan with heated oil
2. Add the cheese, milk and fish
3. Cover and simmer for 8 – 10 minutes, stirring occasionally
4. Stir in the cooked pasta, heat through for 1 – 2 minutes
5. Garnish with Parsley and serve

Lasagne Sauce:

Ingredients:

- 250g Minced Beef
- 1 onion, finely chopped
- 4 small mushrooms or 1 green pepper
- 400g Chopped Tomatoes
- 1 clove of garlic
- 1 stock cube
- 1 tsp mixed herbs
- 1 tbsp Tomato Puree

Method:

1. Finely chop the onion, pepper or mushrooms, and the garlic.
2. Put the mince and vegetables in a pan and cook gently for 5 minutes
3. Mix the chopped tomatoes, stock cube, herbs and puree
4. Bring to the boil and leave to simmer for 10 minutes
5. Place in a container, label and place in the freezer

Equipment:

- Saucepan
- Chopping Board
- Sharp Knife
- Plate

Cheese Sauce:

Ingredients:
- 25g Butter/Margarine
- 2 tbsp Flour
- 400ml Milk
- 75g Cheese
- Salt/Pepper
- $\frac{1}{2}$ tsp Mustard Powder

Equipment:
- Saucepan
- Wooden Spoon
- Grater
- Teaspoon

Method:

1. Put the flour, milk and margarine in a saucepan

2. Slowly heat, stirring all the time with a wooden spoon until it thickens. **Do not allow lumps to form**.

3. Remove pan from heat and add $\frac{3}{4}$ of cheese, stir until melted and smooth

4. Season with salt, pepper and mustard powder

Assembly of Lasagne:

- You need a foil container and you need to layer the lasagne in the following way:
  - $\frac{1}{2}$ Lasagne sauce
  - Layer of Pasta
  - $\frac{1}{2}$ Cheese Sauce
  - Remaining $\frac{1}{2}$ of Lasagne Sauce
  - Layer of Pasta
  - Remaining $\frac{1}{2}$ Cheese Sauce
  - Sprinkle over remaining $\frac{1}{4}$ of Cheese
- Bake in oven: Gas Mark 5/180°C for 25 minutes until golden brown and piping hot.

Parmesan Chicken Nuggets

Ingredients:
- 50g Breadcrumbs
- 1 x 5ml spoon mixed herbs
- 1 x 15 ml spoon parmesan, grated
- 1 – 2 chicken breast
- 1 x 15ml spoon plain flour
- 1 egg beaten

Equipment:
- Baking tray
- Grater
- Small bowl
- Fork
- Knife
- Chopping board

Method:
1. Preheat the oven to 200°C or gas mark 6.
2. Mix the breadcrumbs, herbs and parmesan together in a small bowl.
3. Pour the flour on a small plate.
4. Beat the egg in a small bowl.
5. Cut the chicken into 'nuggets' (approximately 4cm x 3cm chunks).
6. Dust the chicken in the flour.
7. Dip in the beaten egg.
8. Roll in the breadcrumb mixture.
9. Place on the baking tray.
10. Repeat steps 7-10 for all the chicken pieces.
11. Bake in the oven to 20minutes, until golden brown.

Shepard's Pie

Method

Pre prep
Peel the potatoes, peel and dice the carrots and onion, slice the celery (or what ever vegetables you have available).

The mash potato
boil potatoes until soft
Once soft drain the water with a colander and mash with a potato masher adding milk and butter to make the texture creamy, add the sautéed onions when ready.

The vegetables
Place a frying pan on the hob on a medium heat add 50g of butter and the diced onion. Leave to fry till golden in colour (this is called **sauté**), then remove the onions to a plate, **without loosing the oil, add**
Now sauté the other vegetables

The mince
Fry the mince in the frying pan with the oil until brown in colour.

Assembling
Place the mince in your oven bowel, spread the mince evenly across the bottom of the bowel and add the potato mixture on top, finally add the grated cheese and place in the oven to brown on top.

Ingredients:

1lb/500g of potatoes
50g grated cheese
1 medium onion
1 kg mince
150 g butter
100 ml milk
2 carrots
2 sticks of celery

Pasta Salad

Ingredients:
- 100g Cooked Pasta
- 1 Small Onion
- $\frac{1}{2}$ Red/Green Pepper
- Small piece of Cucumber
- 1 tablespoon Sweetcorn
- 1 tablespoon Frozen Garden Peas
- 1 Tin of Tuna, Salmon, Crab, Sardines etc.

Equipment:
- Knife
- Chopping Board
- Tablespoon
- Tin Opener

Method:
1. Peel and finely chop the onion, put in bowl
2. Wash, deseed and the chop the pepper and tomato, put in bowl
3. Wash, slice and dice cucumber, put in bowl with sweetcorn, peas, pasta and salt and pepper
4. Drain fish and add to bowl, mix gently and place in container

Easy Peasy Bread

Ingredients:
- 250g Strong White or Wholemeal Flour
- 1 level teaspoon Salt
- ½ sachet of quick acting yeast
- 150ml warm water
- 1 Tablespoon oil

Equipment:
- Bread Tin
- Measuring jug
- Mixing Bowl
- Flour Dredger
- Wire cooling rack

Method:
1. Grease the bread tin
2. Put flour in a bowl, stir in the yeast and stir in the salt
3. Pour the warm water and oil in to the flour and mix together
4. Knead firmly for ten minutes
5. Place in the bread tin
6. Put in a warm place to rise
7. Bake for 15 – 20 minutes
8. To see if it is cooked tap the underneath and they and they should sound hollow
9. Leave to cool on a wire rack

Making your own pizza

You will make the pizza dough 1 between 2. You need to be quick as time in the lesson is short!

Equipment: (1 between 2)

- 1 Glass Bowl (large)
- 1 measuring jug
- 1 teaspoon
- 1 tablespoon
- 1 spreading knife

Ingredients: (1 between 2)

- 1 bag of flour (250g)
- 1 teaspoon yeast
- 1 teaspoon of salt
- 1 tablespoon of oil
- 150ml warm water

Stage 1:

1. Put the flour, salt and yeast into a large glass bowl and mix with spreading knife.

Stage 2:

1. Place 1 tablespoon of oil in the bowl
2. Add water a little at a time while stirring with spreading knife
3. Continue adding water until the dough is formed (keep stirring with the spreading knife)

Stage 3:

1. Split the dough in half
2. Each person kneads their dough until soft and 'workable'

Stage 4:

1. Make the dough into a circle using your hands
2. Then roll the dough using your rolling pin until it is thin

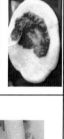

Stage 5:

1. Fold half your pizza base over your rolling pin and transport to your baking sheet

Stage 6:

1. Spoon your pizza topping onto your pizza and spread out evenly
2. Add your toppings and bake in the oven for 10 – 15 minutes

Stage 7:

1. While the pizza is cooking complete all of your washing up.
2. Remember to scrub your tables

Stage 8:

1. Take your pizza out of the oven and allow to cool before putting it in your container
2. Remember to wash your baking sheet!

Printed in Germany
by Amazon Distribution
GmbH, Leipzig